FOR ALL THE PEOPLE

FOR ALL THE PEOPLE

by

DAVID WINTER

HODDER AND STOUGHTON

Printed in Great Britain for Hodder &
Stoughton Limited, St. Paul's House,
Warwick Lane, London E.C.4, by Cox &
Wyman, Limited, London, Fakenham
and Reading

"BEHOLD, I bring you good news of great joy
which will be for all the people"

Contents

Foreword

David Winter, the versatile editor of *Crusade*, has written a splendid book on a splendid theme. He wields his pen with vigour and dips it in humour. And the fascination of his story carries you along as you read. It will not only bring deserved credit under God to the Scripture Union in its Centenary year, but help people to renewed faith in the Bible and in the God of the Bible. Our God is the living God and His Word a living word. If you doubt these things, read the stories in this book, and you will see God at work through His Word convicting, converting, assuring, transforming, challenging, comforting. Yes, and that in the lives of plain, ordinary people too.

I have special and personal reasons for having gladly agreed to contribute this Foreword. The first is that I myself, as a schoolboy of nearly seventeen, was led to Christ by a Scripture Union staff worker. He showed me the way one Sunday afternoon, and that night I knelt at my bedside in the school dormitory and received Christ. This same Scripture Union worker with conscientious persistence nurtured and helped me in the early years of my Christian life, sent me Scripture Union notes (which helped to illumine the Book my mother had taught me to read each day) and gave me my first taste of Christian service two Summers running at the CSSM seaside mission at Borth in Cardiganshire.

Secondly, in my travels in different parts of the world, I have been greatly impressed both by the calibre of Scripture Union staff and by their enterprise. Wherever an opportunity has presented itself, the Scripture Union worker has turned up to take it. One example must do. Some time in 1962 I visited Emmanuel College, Ibadan, Nigeria, to speak to the Anglican and Methodist theological students about evangelism. It was only a brief visit, and only for a single talk. Yet there was the local Scripture Union staff worker, having obtained permission on his own initiative to turn the college library into a temporary bookshop. I remember the crush vividly, as eager students crowded round the table to inspect and buy the books.

Thirdly, I admire very much the way in which this organisation, born in the Victorian era, has kept itself up to date. The Scripture Union richly deserves to be called a "movement", for that is what it is, constantly on the move, adapting and adjusting itself to the demands and opportunities of the day. Its staff members who are known to me personally are men and women of ability, vision and drive. I thank God for the Scripture Union and pray that it may always be kept moving with the times, relating the unchanging gospel to the needs of the contemporary world.

John R. W. Stott

Introduction

It all began with her picking up *Woman's Own*. Different lives have different turning points with different causes, but a casual half-hour with a woman's magazine seems as unlikely a turning point as any. Yet that is just what it was.

She turned the pages, and came across a column by David Sheppard, the cricketer-parson. In it he argued the value of regular daily Bible reading, and recommended the use of the Scripture Union method and notes. Now Mrs Grant— that's not her real name, but it will do—was not a practising Christian, nor was she familiar with the Bible. But she decided to do something about it. So she got hold of a set of Scripture Union notes.

Quite on her own, with no encouragement or advice from anybody else, she kept up this habit of regular, daily Bible reading for two years, when her husband decided to join her. A few months later a new Baptist church was opened in their district. Mrs Grant decided to attend the opening service—and on that very day was converted to faith in Jesus Christ. A month later her husband was converted and within four months they had both been baptised. Four months after that Mrs Grant's mother, to whom she had introduced Scripture Union notes, was also converted.

This completely true story illustrates, in a way chapters of introduction could not explain, what this book is about.

Although it is written for the centenary of the Scripture Union, it is not "a book about SU". It is, in fact, about people and the Bible; the Bible and people: just that. Of course, our special theme is the way God has used the Scripture Union, in all its different facets, to bring people and Bible together. But our hope is that the SU will be seen as simply a catalyst: an ingredient whose presence makes action and reaction possible.

The Scripture Union, just a hundred years old, has been a long while in the "people and Bible" business.* Launched in 1867 by a slightly eccentric gentleman called Josiah Spiers, it began life as a seaside mission to children—and that work remains to this day. Ten years later the Scripture Union scheme of daily Bible reading was born. This century has seen schools work (through the Inter-School Christian Fellowship), Sunday school teacher training, large-scale publishing in the youth and children's field and international developments all over the world.

The name is the same, more or less. But today a million and a quarter people all over the world are engaged on daily Bible reading "the SU way"—and heaven alone knows how many more people are reached for God through the Bible by other SU activities. The London headquarters—a large office block in Marylebone and one of London's largest bookshops a block or two away—is now the hub of a very considerable machine. But the machine has a heart, and that heart is the Gospel itself.

The Bible is the people's book. God gave it to them, for them. It is not primarily a book of philosophies, theories

---

* It began under the name "Children's Special Service Mission", later becoming the "CSSM and Scripture Union".

or propositions; but a book about relationships—between God and man, and between man and his fellow. In the Bible God speaks: to human hearts, to human needs, to human dilemmas. This is a *living* book, because the Holy Spirit who inspired its human authors is still active inspiring its human readers and applying its truths to their lives.

At various periods in history people have rejected the Bible. Indeed, the last eighty years have seen it suffer attack and ridicule enough to sink any other literary work in history. But the Bible, like a cork in a basin, always bobs up again. It cannot be suppressed; it cannot even easily be ignored.

It is through the Word of God—the message of God to men, found today in the pages of the Bible—that men are born anew into God's kingdom.* It is through the Word of God that new-born Christians grow.† Through the Bible God guides, directs, corrects and reproves, encourages and commissions His people.‡

But today many people are ignorant of its message. Bored by unimaginative "Scripture" lessons at school, perhaps, or daunted by having attempted to read an Authorised Version Bible without help, they have decided the Bible is "not for them". *But it is.* God gave it, like the land, to the people. It was left to men to complicate it, obscure it and make it respectable and dull. It is the task of the Scripture Union and the CSSM, and has been for a century, to uncomplicate the Bible, throw light on its meaning, and make it practical, relevant and *real* for the ordinary reader.

* I Peter 1: 23.
† I Peter 2: 2.
‡ 2 Tim. 3: 15–17

This book is not only about people, but it is very largely *by* them, too. The people whose stories it tells are mostly quite ordinary folk, in ordinary situations—seeking God, doubting God, having personal problems and sorrows and trials, needing help and comfort—who have found that through the Bible God has spoken to them.

It is their book really: an anthology about people and God and this very remarkable book, the Bible—the book which the British coronation service describes as "the most precious thing this world affords".

CHAPTER I

For People in Search of God

"I'm sorry it had to be like this, Johnny, honestly I am. You know that, don't you?"

Johnny nodded glumly, the light from the street lamp catching on the top rim of his glasses.

"I've tried, you know I have . . . but there's no other answer. It's not that I'm not very fond of you, Johnny . . ."

"I don't get it," Johnny said softly, looking at her for the first time during the conversation—pained, baffled, hurt. "I don't get it. Just because you're religious, and I'm not! I wouldn't interfere, I might even become a Christian one day . . . what does it matter?"

"A lot . . . much more than you think. Everything. The world, really."

There was an awkward moment's silence. There was nothing more to say, but neither wanted to be the one to walk away. For months they had both seen this coming—Rita's conscience telling her that as a Christian she must not become too deeply attached to a boy who was an agnostic; John's irritation at her groundless scruples, as though he were some sort of a moral leper. And now, the rending moment of leave-taking.

Rita put her hand in the pocket of her coat, more as a

gesture than to find anything, and felt the New Testament she had been given as a Christmas present.

"Here, Johnny," she said, on an impulse, pushing it into his hands. "You read that. You'll find the answers there— all of them."

Before he could comment, or hand it back, she had turned on her heel and disappeared into the pool of darkness between their lamp-post and the next one.

Johnny took the New Testament home with him and before getting into bed that night opened it and began to read. After all, it could do no harm.

It was a modern version—the Revised Standard—and quite easy going. John found himself caught up in it, and read on beyond midnight. In the space of thirty-six hours he had read it through, and the effect on him had been dynamic.

Sensing that he was at a turning-point in his life, captive to the spell of good news, he immediately began to re-read it: Matthew, Mark, Luke—and then, while reading through John's Gospel, it happened. Suddenly shattered by the majesty and love of Christ, he knelt down and received Him as his Saviour.

Now it wouldn't be fair or accurate to call that story typical: most people come to Christ in much less spectacular ways. But it does illustrate the tremendous power and authority of the Bible and its message. The customer who bought that New Testament in the Scripture Union's London bookshop could not possibly have foretold its transforming effect on Johnny; yet it was simply the buying and passing on of a book which brought him to the most momentous step of his young life.

Usually God uses people to bring other people to Himself, but nevertheless the story of Johnny is by no means unique. Plenty of others have had no guide, no evangelist and no counsellor but the Bible up to the time of their conversion.

Take Paul and Joseph Weldon, for instance: two brothers from Australia. Both ardent idealists, they set out after the War to promote a movement to bring the best elements of all religions together in a great, worldwide movement of peace and hope.

It was no crazy dream, either. With tremendous zeal they got the backing of many of the world's religious leaders, and very large numbers of influential people gave them their support. They travelled across the world and came to London. Then Paul, who had been involved in an accident in Australia, was injured again and further travel was out of the question. He became a shut-in. Largely because time hung on his hands, but also because they suddenly became aware that they knew very little indeed of the Bible's contents, although they were such keen promoters of "religion", they determined to find out exactly what the Bible had to say.

All day Paul would read it, making notes. Then, in the evenings, Joseph would join him and they would discuss the day's study.

The result was dramatic indeed. It was the story of Nicodemus (John 3) which brought things to a head. This deeply religious man—"a teacher of Israel"—was very much like they were. Yet Jesus told him that unless a man was "born of the Spirit" he could not see the Kingdom of heaven.

17

Weeks of Bible study, Old and New Testament, suddenly began to click into place. Christ was the sacrifice, the ransom for sin. When men put their trust in Him they were born again into a new life, a new kingdom, a new world. This transformation was an inner, spiritual thing, with outward practical results: and without it none could really be called "Christian".

There and then the two brothers responded to Christ and took Him at His word. The result has been the founding of a remarkable little work of evangelism by these two men (Paul is still more or less bed-ridden) and a tremendous influence for Christ in hundreds of lives. Yet, these two men—religious, satisfied, sensitive—were brought to the Saviour simply and solely through the Bible. Human help and fellowship, in their case, came much later.

As Joseph has put it, "There was no Jesus Christ present in our room for our Nicodemus, no Philip for our Ethiopian problems: in fact, for us 'there was no man'. We were on our own—or so we thought in our ignorance! *But we had a book*, and the book that contained the problems must also contain the solutions. We had dug deep before in other contexts; we would dig again, and keep on until we had resolved these matters."

The Bible is for people—people who are groping their way to faith; and people who have lost the faith they once had. This is part of a letter sent on to the Scripture Union a few years ago:

"For some time now either your office or some enthusiast for your work has been sending me a copy of the *Missionary Messenger* and the *Daily Notes* of the Scripture Union. For some time I ignored both, for I am what keener Christians would call a complete backslider from any kind of Christian profession, though brought up in a home where formal religion was practised after a fashion. But on Wednesday, July 5th, my wife, who is of Jewish extraction, picked up the *Daily Notes* and was struck by the thought that Christianity and the Jewish faith were complementary and not antagonistic, as she had been taught to believe. Somehow the interest spread, so that before a week had passed, we read them together from a school Bible, and, instructed by the comments of the writer of the *Notes*, we became increasingly conscious that the message of the Bible and the pithy comments were something we both needed, but had hitherto missed. Finally, on Wednesday the 26th, my wife and I knew that we could no longer delay the issue, and on the strength of the passage for the day (Matthew 11: 25–30) and the explanation appended, trusted God for a real Christian experience, and it has worked. When our two sons returned from the University on vacation we told them what we had done, wondering what their reactions would be. To our astonishment one of them told us he, too, had been given the same *Notes* and had been reading them with interest. Suffice it to say here that both our boys, and our daughter, training for a teaching post abroad, have been truly converted, and so our hearts are overwhelmed at it all. My wife's parents are very interested. I have given them the same *Notes* on St Matthew because they seem to be particularly suitable to their minds.

"In three days' time we will all be sailing to Cape Town, but felt that before leaving to take up an executive post in engineering we should inform you of these facts which mean so much to us, and for which we are indebted to you or one of your supporters.

"Wishing you great success in spreading over the world the only message that could have got under the skin of such as we are, and which has done us so much good . . ."

Here again is the Bible speaking: not in the isolated words of a verse superstitiously torn from its context, but through its total message, the overwhelming impact of sheer truth. This is its primary task—to shine light into darkness, to bring life to places of death. It is by the "living and abiding word of God" that men are born again into Christ's kingdom. As we shall see it has many other tasks in the divine scheme, but it is the Word of God that the Holy Spirit normally uses to break through the crust of indifference or opposition in the human heart. This is true of those who know nothing of God, and of those who lack nothing where religion is concerned but a living faith.

Sometimes, of course, it *is* one verse. A mother of three girls looks back to the day when the light of Christ first really dawned in her life. Brought up in a Christian home but, at thirteen, lacking a really personal faith, she was reading her Scripture Union passage before going to bed. She read Ezekiel 36: 26 — "A new heart I will give you, and a new spirit I will put within you . . ."—and, in her own words, "the light of God's truth suddenly dawned upon me in an unmistakable manner". Not many come to faith in quite such an instantaneous and clear-cut way, but for those who do the transition from doubt to assurance, from indecision to commitment, is not only sudden but complete.

Probably most often a person's journey into faith is a complex of actions and reactions, involving other people, the Church, conscience, events and, almost invariably, the Bible.

A young typist tells how she came to God. Nineteen years old, "quite normal" (in her own words), a two or three times a year churchgoer, she came into contact with a "real" Christian for the first time in her life. This was a person who spoke about God and Jesus and trust in Him. "Why, he even mentioned the devil as though he were a real person! I remember quite distinctly sitting at my typewriting desk one coffee break trying hard not to smile."

But she was disturbed, uneasy. Does God really want us to come to know Him personally in Jesus Christ? She bought a Bible and started reading it. Her Christian colleague suggested she should use the Scripture Union method. For the first time in her life—there had been abortive attempts at Bible reading before—she not only read the Scriptures but found them speaking to her, meaning things, bringing life. Faith followed, but truth led the way.

It must be faced that stories of people being converted to faith in Christ simply through reading the Bible, though impressive as testimonies to the Bible's inherent authority and dynamism, are nevertheless abnormal, in the true sense of that word. When Philip ran alongside the chariot in which an Ethiopian was reading to himself from the book of Isaiah —the story is in Acts 8—his question was, "Do you understand what you are reading?" The Ethiopian's answer was another question "How can I, unless somebody helps me?" This is the normal. The Bible and Christian history testify to the fact that the Bible's message and human, personal explanation of it go hand in hand in the vast majority of conversions to Christ.

It was like that with Nigel Goodwin (for once, that is his real name). Nigel was a young actor, RADA-trained, full of bounce and confidence, and just making his way towards the upper levels of his profession. From scene-shifting and walk-on parts he had graduated to regular leads in repertory and then to a number of good roles in television drama.

So far as he can remember, God and the Bible had played little part in his life. Certainly he seldom thought about them. His West End flat, his show-business friends and his stage and TV work were the three sides of a full and quite satisfying life.

Nigel's mother and sister, however, had become Christians, and occasionally tried to persuade him to sample the less heady joys of an evangelistic meeting or two. But this fish was not falling for the bait. Nigel had a shrewd suspicion that once one got committed in this sphere it was particularly hard to get uncommitted. Also he had a sneaking suspicion that they were praying for him, and anyone who has been "prayed for" will know how very vulnerable he now felt.

And yet, in fact, he did accept an invitation of theirs—to attend a meeting in (of all things) a tent on (of all places) Wimbledon Common. It was, in fact, part of the CSSM "Inland Mission" held there each Summer.

The strange initials CSSM stand for Children's Special Service Mission (and it's just as well Nigel didn't know *that*)—it is in fact the parent body of what is now officially entitled the Scripture Union movement. Originally it confined its activities to seaside missions for children of the upper classes, and then beach missions on a wider basis;

but the 1960's saw it launching out into inland missions for children and young people as well.

It was to this rather unlikely mission meeting that Nigel came, reluctantly, defiantly, inquisitively. He sat with his mother and sister and watched the leaders endure a torrent of abuse, ridicule, back-chat and ordinary cheek from a noisy crowd of irreverent youngsters. The incredible thing, as Nigel saw it, was that they seemed to take it all in good part. Nobody on the platform lost his temper. Nobody even seemed very worried. They simply continued quietly with what they had to say, smiling and just taking whatever came their way.

Nigel was impressed. He knew something about hostile audiences, "getting the bird" and ignoring interruptions. But this was different. They were not covering seething anger or blank despair with brave faces. These Christians did not seem to worry very much. All they cared about—a fool could see this—was that the youngsters should find what they had found: peace and purpose.

Above the din it was hard to follow what was said, but Nigel agreed to attend another meeting a couple of days later. This time the interruptions were less intrusive, and he was able to follow quite easily as the speaker outlined from the Bible the way in which people can come to God through His Son, and be accepted, forgiven and made new by Him. Impressed as much by the people themselves as by what they said, Nigel was acutely aware of a moment of spiritual crisis as the meeting drew to a close. As it ended he sought out the leader, Arthur Page, and there and then committed his own life to Jesus Christ.

The Bible, Christian witness, a sincere seeker: here is the

true trinity of evangelism, the ideal setting for the Holy Spirit to do His work of drawing men and women to the Saviour.

The way in which Sir Alfred Owen, one of Britain's leading industrialists, came to faith in Christ illustrates this fact.

He had just inherited his father's industrial empire, a bewildered undergraduate saddled with vast responsibilities. A friend took him to a Christian Union sermon in Holy Trinity church, Cambridge – and he might have responded on the spot had an over-earnest student not tackled him immediately after the service and told him he was "lost". He fought against the Gospel—successfully, until the end of term.

During the vacation he began to read the Bible, using a set of Scripture Union notes written by Dr Graham Scroggie. For the first time he began to question the liberal view of the Bible which he had unquestioningly accepted since public school-days. Then, early the next term, Scroggie himself came to Cambridge to preach and Owen went to hear him. It was then that his friend's witness, the impact of the Bible itself, and the powerful application of its truth from the pulpit combined to break down his resistance. "Shaking at the knees", as he put it in a newspaper article,* he walked up the aisle of Holy Trinity outwardly to confess his faith in Jesus Christ.

A similar story, only spread over a much longer period of time, is that of a housewife looking back over a long pilgrimage to faith, covering a period of some fifteen years.

It began with a wartime holiday at Westward Ho, when

* *Church of England Newspaper.* November 5th 1965.

six years old Gillian joined in the activities of a CSSM beach mission. She won first prize for beach modelling—a scenic layout with farms, lanes, corn-fields, woods and so on. Because of this she had to go to the prize-giving service a day or two later. Although she can recall with great clarity her sand scene, she cannot recollect anything that was said or sung at the meeting, but she was put on a mailing list, at her own request, for Scripture Union notes.

Faithfully the anonymous provider sent the notes for the next seven years. Gillian read some but more often forgot them until they made her Bible bulge. Then she threw them away.

At twelve she went away to boarding school. There she got a good dose of traditional English school religion, plenty of music, ceremony and vigour. She "joined the bandwagon of annual confirmations" and finally left school "ignorant, untaught, lazy" and pretty proud of her regular church attendance—and yet, on her own confession, utterly lost, empty. She began to look for herself into the truth of things. She remembered the SU notes and decided to read a little of the Bible every day.

Lost emotionally—"I had scattered, at nineteen, my affections in several different directions at once"—lost socially and lost geographically in the wilderness of London, where she made a mess of her training as a nurse, she was now aware of positive dangers in her situation.

At that critical moment in life she accepted an invitation by some of the other nurses to join a camp they were attending. There Gillian heard, for the first time consciously, the simple clear message of Christ in His own words, and took by faith the first hesitant step in response to the love of God

—the first step towards Christian maturity and Christian motherhood.

"You have been born anew," wrote the apostle Peter, "not of perishable seed, but of imperishable, through the living and abiding word of God." Only a living word could so perfectly adapt to the needs and situations of so many different people; only an abiding word—that is, a word that is reliable, substantial, not subject to change—could offer people in need a sure and certain hope.

The work of the Scripture Union and CSSM, in all its different aspects, could be described as bringing this unchanging, reliable and yet living word to as many people as possible. This means that Scripture Union, like the book it handles, has to be at the same time faithful and unchanging in what it has to say, and yet infinitely adaptable and resourceful in the way it says it. So a whole ministry of the "Word" has grown up, with world-wide ramifications, aimed at applying the Bible to every possible human situation and need.

Most of the people we have mentioned so far have been British, and in most cases the Bible itself, the witness of Christian men and women, and circumstances of need have combined to bring them to faith in Christ. Beyond that we have not yet looked (though later on we shall).

But in some cases, especially where the SU's overseas work is concerned, to open one's mind to God's Word, and respond to it, is to place oneself in a position of very real sacrifice and even danger.

Jag Kenth is an example of this. He was a Sikh from near Ludhiana, in the Punjab. In obedience to his religion he always wore his turban over his long hair, and, as he got older, he also grew quite a respectable beard. The Sikh, of course, never cuts his hair or shaves.

While Jag Kenth was still at school, his parents moved to East Africa, where his mother died, and he was brought up by his father, who was in business there.

However, when he was sixteen or so his father sent him back to India to get an "English" education, and especially to pass his Cambridge exam at an English-speaking school. He was enrolled in a Christian school, and as a condition of attendance he had to go to Scripture classes and to church—despite his strong objections.

Nevertheless, whether he liked it or not, he came to know what the Christian Gospel was about. An able young man, he was made vice-captain of the school—a position he held at the time that a Scripture Union/CSSM worker, the Rev. Cecil Johnston, came to the school to conduct a mission. During the mission Jag Kenth was deeply moved. What he had heard in class and what he now heard from the missioner made a devastating impact on him. Towards the end of the mission he asked for a personal talk with Mr Johnston, and finally surrendered his life to Jesus Christ.

At a Scripture Union camp which he attended soon after, where there were also many boys from his school, including a number of other Sikhs and Hindus, Jag Kenth stood up boldly and told them that he had become a Christian, that he intended to be baptised, and —most dramatically of all—to have his beard shaved off. It was this last action that would inevitably cut him off from his own race and even his own family.

He wrote to his father in East Africa telling him of the steps that he was taking. Not surprisingly father was extremely angry and wrote a furious letter begging the boy not to take this step and warning him of the consequences if he did. He would be disinherited and disowned by the whole family. Jag Kenth was very distressed to get this letter—though he had guessed his father's reaction—but held firm, and told his father that nothing could shake his resolve to be baptised.

Father next tried more devious methods. He wrote saying that he was very ill, and must see his son soon. Jag Kenth packed his bags at once and—still unbaptised—set off for East Africa. Back at home the threats and pleadings continued, but he held firm, taking a job as a teacher and trying to live as a Christian at home, with love and without bitterness.

In time his father began to soften, and became more or less reconciled to the fact that Jag meant what he said. The young man had the opportunity to come to Britain, and took it. As soon as he arrived in London he joined a church and was baptised on September 12th 1965. Even getting started on the Christian pilgrimage was a long process for Jag Kenth, but his story illustrates the truth that once that "living and abiding word" gets planted in a man's spirit it is not easily rooted out.

This chapter has been concerned with the infinite variety of ways in which the Holy Spirit uses the Bible, and, of course, in these cases also the particular ministry of the Scripture Union, to bring men and women from unbelief to faith. We have seen how the simple, regular reading of the Bible has been used—and also the sudden impact of a single statement of Scripture; the witness of a friend at work, or of a set of Scripture reading notes; or the work of a human agent of God, like the SU missioner referred to above, or the preacher whose writings and sermon so shattered the young undergraduate Alfred Owen.

Perhaps we could end this chapter with one more instance of the power of the Scriptures, almost entirely without personal contact with Christians, to speak to a person and bring them to Christ. It is the story of a woman whom we shall call Mrs Brown.

She had been deserted by her husband, leaving her with three small children. On top of this she had to go into hospital for an operation. Subsequently she was sent to a convalescent home, where a simple service was held for the patients each week. There was obviously some hunger for God in her heart, because she not only enjoyed the service very much, but was disappointed when the speaker did not give his hearers a clear explanation of the exact way in which one could become a Christian. But when she left the convalescent home the Sister gave her some Scripture Union notes. When she got home she began to read the Bible regularly, even writing to Scripture Union headquarters to order further notes when the ones she had expired. For two or three years this continued. She never went to church, and had no real contact with any Christians, but she faithfully and carefully read the Bible every day. One is forced to wonder how many thousands of people there may well be like her up and down the British Isles.

Her children went to Sunday school at the local Baptist church, and one of the teachers suggested to the minister that he should call on Mrs Brown. It was a "routine visit" he will not forget in a hurry.

In the course of trying to make helpful conversation, the

minister mentioned that he personally had found reading the Bible a great help in his daily life. He was somewhat taken aback when Mrs Brown walked over to the bookcase, pulled out her Bible, and showed him the Scripture Union notes tucked in the pages at that day's reading. She told him that she had been reading the Bible for more than two years, and explained about her experience in hospital.

The minister asked her if she had ever become a Christian. She replied in words very similar to those of the Ethiopian eunuch (Acts 8: 31), that she wanted to, but "no-one had ever helped her except the sister at the convalescent home".

"I asked her if she would like to receive Christ," the minister relates, "and started to explain the way of salvation. I found her one who, as a result of reading the Scripture Union portion regularly, had such a clear understanding of God's way that my words were hardly necessary." They knelt down there and then—in front of her children—and she received Jesus Christ as her Lord and Saviour.

I said that Mrs Brown came to faith "almost entirely without personal contact" with Christians. In fact that is only half the truth. It was the Bible, and the Bible only, that lit up her mind and heart and revealed to her the Son of God. But it was human agents who, guided by the Holy Spirit, first recorded the truth of God in the Scriptures. It was human agents who copied it down the ages and preserved the text. It was human agents who translated it into English, who selected the daily readings for the Scripture Union and who wrote the notes. It was a human agent—the hospital Sister—who first encouraged Mrs Brown to open her Bible and start reading it, and another human, the writer of the SU notes, who helped her understand what she read. It was yet another human, the Baptist minister, who introduced her to Jesus Christ, and then to His Church, and who baptised her a few months later.

It is this perfect interaction of human and divine which characterises the Christian faith, which has at its heart a Redeemer who is both truly human and fully divine. When you have grasped all the implications of Mrs Brown's journey into faith, then you will have also grasped the heart of the Scripture Union's ministry: to bring the word of Christ to people, all·people, everywhere; and people, all people, everywhere, to the Christ of the Word.

CHAPTER 2

For Young People

A few rows of red-faced village children fidgetted on the hard forms. The hall was dark, darker than usual, and filled with a funny smell of carbide gas. On a temporary screen hung on the wall a succession of gaudily coloured and grossly over-drawn scenes from *Pilgrim's Progress* jerked into sight and then jerked away again. The busiest man in the building was the perspiring evangelist of the Caravan Mission, who had the exhausting task of keeping the "magic lantern" going (a major feat on its own), inserting the slides in the correct order and the right way up, at the same time providing a commentary lucid and gripping enough to hold the attention of twenty or thirty youngsters more used to fresh air and open fields.

Still, despite their giggles as the earnest preacher scorched his fingers or inserted Giant Despair head first, the children enjoyed these visits. As well as the magic lantern (and magic it seemed, in those days before electricity had reached the villages of rural England) they had choruses, Bible games and object talks.

One boy, Stanley, was certainly deeply impressed. "One evening," he recalls, "it came to me very forcefully that if Pilgrim in the story had a big burden, difficult to dispose of, then if I did not receive Jesus Christ while I was young I might well find myself later in the same plight." So it was that that night he responded to the grace of God and gave his life to Christ. "It was simple, yet sincere. And though in some respects I did not show any revolutionary change, I did become increasingly aware of the fact of this change."

Stanley was then thirteen. Quite soon he was church organist, then a Sunday school teacher. Bible school followed, when he was twenty, and today he is himself an evangelist with the Caravan Mission. This Mission, incidentally, is another branch of the work of the Scripture Union. Stanley's story, quite "normal" of its kind, helps to show how effective the movement's work can be and has been amongst children and young people.

This is not surprising in an organisation born out of meetings for children on a seaside beach. Today the Scripture Union and CSSM carries on work amongst the young at many different levels: seaside missions for all ages from toddlers up to teen-agers; the CMVC work in rural areas; the Inter-School Christian Fellowship, in touch with Christian groups in two thousand schools all over Britain; work in Borstals and Approved Schools; camps and house-parties for boys and girls from boarding schools; yachting cruises on the Broads for schoolboys and girls, and literature at every level, from comics to sixth-form handbooks.

Some readers may wonder whether it is possible for small children—under secondary school age—to have a true experience of "conversion". The author would have to confess that he himself had the gravest doubts on this score before researching for this book. But the sheer weight of testimony has impressed me that young children, given wise

33

a

handling, experienced teachers and an unemotional, simple approach, can not only have a transparently real experience of Christ, but also one that lasts a life-time.

"I accepted Jesus Christ as my Saviour when eleven years old at a CSSM meeting at Margate," writes an elderly lady who is now secretary of a Scripture Union group scattered all over the world.

"It was at a Scripture Union meeting for children on September 15th 1891 that I decided for Christ," writes a lady in North London, "and I am still a member of the Scripture Union". A large but unascertainable body of assorted bishops, clergy, ministers, evangelists and eminent lay Christians could tell similar stories.

A glance through a file of brief case histories kept by a Scripture Union children's evangelist confirms this impression.

"P.L. Trusted the Lord Jesus in November 1950 one month before his ninth birthday. No spectacular progress for some time, then after camping with us for a few years blossomed out into a wonderful experience of the Lord. Worked with BBC TV, and then resigned because of Sunday work and is now with a large radio firm . . . With his wife, is doing a wonderful work at his parish church."

"P.T. Converted at the age of eleven through a tent mission in his village in 1949. A very brainy chap who won a scholarship to Cambridge and got an honours degree in Science . . . works on atomic energy research . . . doing useful Christian service in home and district."

"N.B. Converted at camp six or seven years ago. Fine leader of the Christian Union in his grammar school . . .

now an electrical engineer. I hear fine reports of his work as a Methodist local preacher."

"C.B. A very unattractive little girl of 12 who lived in an isolated village. Attended two missions in the chapel in August 1943 and the following January. At the latter meetings responded to the Lord's call ... Married in 1955 a very keen Christian serving with the American Air Force . . . teaches in the local school."

"L.B. Converted as a boy of twelve in a tent mission. . . Now the mainstay of the local Methodist church."

It is also confirmed by the follow-up lists of the seaside missions. One which has been kept up over a period of years, relating to just one resort, includes the names of one bishop, more than twenty men ordained in one denomination or another, twenty-four missionaries and a good number of others whose names are well-known in Church life.

It must be conceded, of course, that many child "conversions" do not last. But this is true of "conversions" at any age. It is also true of candidates for confirmation and adult baptism. Careful research does not suggest any significant difference in the percentage of those who "fall away" amongst small children as compared with teenagers or young adults.

It must also be conceded that there has been plenty of ill-advised "evangelism" amongst small children, much of it by soul-hunting evangelists working more for a mention in the Christian press than for entries in the Book of Life. But such men are not to be found on the staff of responsible bodies like the Scripture Union. Wise evangelists amongst children know how to build from the foundations upwards, with a firm basis of Christian teaching supporting a simple but profound love for Jesus Christ and trust in Him.

This love and trust normally comes most easily to those who have had the priceless advantage of a Christian home and the care and prayer of a Christian church. One rather unusual story along these lines tells of a young girl in a vicarage family long ago.

"When I was about eight or nine," she writes, "a Scripture Union van, under the direction of a Mr Hewlett, came to our village. My father, who was the vicar, welcomed them and gave them the freedom of the school house for meetings. I never forgot the simple gospel messages given.

"Although not 'high church', our life as children was rigidly regimented. Family prayers, half an hour's Bible reading after breakfast, church twice on Sundays, and the *fear* of God deeply implanted in our minds, with rigid Sabbath observances—it was a sin to pick a flower on Sunday!

"I longed to be a Christian, but didn't know how. Christianity seemed to be all religious observances.

"Then, when I was fifteen, I went for a holiday to Paignton, where—by God's leading, I am sure—Mr Hewlett was conducting beach services, which I attended. The next day his helper, a Mr Bird, met me on the beach and asked me if I were 'converted'. I said I wanted to be but didn't know how, and in a few simple words he showed me it was just a matter of acceptance. Then he took me to Mr Hewlett, and I felt I had been led to that meeting by God."

Quite apart from the fascinating glimpse of life in a country parsonage at the turn of the century, this story shows the value of a ministry designed for the express purpose of making the liberating Word of God available and meaningful to children. It also eloquently answers the allegation that the evangelical experience of conversion is a narrowing, confining thing. Here, as in every true conversion, the effect was of liberation and light.

One must also note that here, as so often, there was no sudden, swift step from darkness to light, but a process, begun, one imagines, in that godly if slightly daunting home and completed by the simple application of the Gospel truths on a Devon beach. The wise children's evangelist only seeks to find the part the possibly very small part— that he is to play in the intimate and gradual work of God in a young life, and to fulfil it carefully and sympathetically.

A good example of this approach is provided by this report from a CMVC evangelist of an incident during a village mission in the War which has had long-term results.

"During that campaign a one-night circus came to the village and all the children went off to it except one boy, Peter. He turned up all on his own, so we spent the evening singing choruses and talking. At one point I asked him if he had accepted the Lord Jesus as his Saviour. 'No,' he replied, 'but I would like to'. I turned him to various passages of Scripture and then we knelt down and he very simply asked the Saviour to come into his life and cleanse it and keep him. That was the beginning of great things for Peter."

Peter was ten when he accepted Christ. Now he is a secondary school teacher running a flourishing Christian group in his school—"I don't know *how* many he has led to the Saviour" comments the evangelist—and a most effective lay preacher, especially to children and young people.

It may well be asked what the appeal of these missions and meetings is to the children. After all, going to religious gatherings is hardly a normal childish pastime, and many of those whose stories I have recorded obviously found normal Church activities rather tedious or else beyond them. The story of another John, although the relevant part of it took place quite a long while ago, may provide part of the answer, for it highlights the relevance and realism of what the CSSM beach missions set out to do.

John was thirteen, an average sort of schoolboy, but rather lonely because he had no brothers or sisters and his mother had died when he was five. He was on holiday at a Scottish seaside resort for the second time. On his previous visit he had spent almost every afternoon and evening at the open-air pierrot show, and, so far as he could see, this second holiday would be passed in much the same way.

In those days many, perhaps most, people on holiday still went to church. As John left church after the service on the first Sunday of his holiday a friendly young man handed him an invitation to a meeting for schoolboys to be held that evening—part of the programme of the Children's Special Service Mission, of which he had vaguely heard from a friend who had been along to it the previous summer.

At home John never went to Sunday school. Just occasionally he went to church on Sunday mornings, but never in the evenings, as Sunday was the day for visiting relations. As there was nothing much to do on holiday on a Sunday evening in those days, he went to the meeting.

It was unlike anything he had ever experienced before.

He learned short hymns called choruses, which had catchy tunes, and listened to a talk which "went to his heart". He also met other members of the CSSM team, and was invited along to the morning service the next day.

Monday morning found John walking slowly along the sands towards the red banner and the gathering crowd, slowly because he was shy and everybody else seemed to know everybody else and exactly what was happening. He cannot recollect today exactly what took place, but it made a sufficient impression to ensure that from that day until the mission ended, and he stood on the station platform waving good-bye tearfully to the men who had become his friends, he never missed one event on the programme for which he was eligible—whether it was a service, a meeting, a game or a competition.

At one of these activities, called a "squash" (presumably, he deduced, because the room was jammed with boys), he heard a talk on the words in the Epistle to Timothy, "Christ Jesus came into the world to save sinners". It moved him profoundly (writing of it now he says, "God's Spirit convicted me concerning my need of a Saviour", but thirteen year olds do not usually express themselves in those terms!) and at the close of the meeting, when all the boys were kneeling in prayer, he got down by an old sofa in the corner and asked Jesus Christ to be his Saviour.

On another occasion at the morning service he filled in a plain form, paid twopence, and received a very Victorian looking Scripture Union card (which set out the daily Bible readings). He did not use it very much, he confesses, but every Christmas thereafter for forty years the leader of that mission sent him a new card. His persistence was not in vain,

for the schoolboy John became a student and the student a
children's evangelist, and the evangelist an ordinand.
Through all this time—and subsequently during his
ministry, and in his home and family life—the book to
which he was introduced at a beach mission long ago has
been the guide and sustainer of his Christian discipleship.

Now that mission was long ago, true. But it would not be
possible to relate its long-term effects, and the durability of
John's conversion, if it were more recent. The approach at
these beach missions has been modernised, of course. The
music, the sports and social events, the terminology: these
have all changed. But the basic objective and method has not
and the appeal of these beach missions—almost incredibly,
in view of the competition from commercially backed holiday entertainments and diversions—has not declined. There
may be rather fewer of them than fifty years ago, but now
they are more highly organised, reaching a far wider range
of children from all sections of society. And still today
children and youngsters say that religion and church
have "come alive" through these special campaigns and
missions.

In fairness one also ought to add that the churches themselves, and especially the Sunday schools, have "come
alive" to the importance of properly organised children's
work. Largely because of the work of the Scripture Union
and CSSM's Sunday School Department, and similar work
by other agencies, the inside of most Sunday schools is
infinitely brighter, and the teaching infinitely better and
more arresting, than they were even fifteen years ago.
Thousands of Sunday school teachers have attended training
courses run by the SU, thousands more have learned the

basics of teaching method from SU literature and film-strips, and hundreds of thousands of children each week are taught from courses planned and devised by the talented and highly experienced staff of the SU and CSSM Sunday school department.

That particular department is also involved in the *Adventurers* "take-home" comic, which includes Bible stories, puzzles and "things to do". A story which begins with *Adventurers* will also serve to illustrate the way in which Christian ministry among children is a most effective way of reaching adults too.

Three children in a Glasgow Sunday school used to take home *Adventurers* each week. Finding the Bible puzzles a bit beyond them, they turned to father for help. He was embarrassed to find that he could not answer most of the questions himself, and, largely through these puzzles and having to look up the answers in the Bible, the father came to a real faith in Christ.

This began a chain reaction in the family. Mother went with a party from the church to a convention, and there she was converted. The difference in the home became so marked that the couple's parents started to take note. After a few months grandpa was converted and soon after grandma, who had been a rather indecisive Christian, came to real assurance of faith. The husband and wife quickly grew to Christian maturity, and now between them run a flourishing Bible class for young people.

Work among very young children is only one aspect of the SU's ministry to youth, however. Probably nothing the movement does is more important, strategically, than the Inter-School Christian Fellowship. This is basically a fellowship of school Christian unions, touching over two thousand secondary schools and through them great numbers of future Christian leaders. Its growth since the Second World War has been one of the most encouraging aspects of post-war Christian witness.

The heart of the work of the ISCF is the individual Christian union meeting in the school. Such meetings defy analysis. They vary from the large, superbly organised group of fifty or sixty fifth and sixth formers, confidently led by mature Christian pupils, with unobtrusive guidance and encouragement from Christian teachers, to the struggling group of five or six meeting for Bible study and prayer.

The contribution from the SU to this work is considerable. Experienced travelling staff help and advise the school groups, run conferences and training evenings for leaders, train boys and girls for group leadership, sixth form conferences seek to relate the Christian faith to pressing current problems, and books, pamphlets and the magazine *Viewpoint* provide tools for the job. New developments include courses for sixth formers in various specialist subjects, such as chemistry, biology or French, when highly qualified Christian tutors not only add depth to the pupils' knowledge of their subjects, but also relate them to the Christian faith and its expression in daily life.

The general pattern of a Christian union in a grammar or modern school is fairly consistent. A small committee of senior pupils runs it, normally with the background assistance of one or two sympathetic teachers. The programme usually includes a weekly or fortnightly meeting. Discussion, Bible study and the occasional visiting speaker make up the programme. The leaders can call on the regional ISCF staff member for advice and guidance, and can share in leaders' conferences and use the literature produced by ISCF. Many who led school Christian groups as boys and girls in the early days have chosen the teaching profession as their Christian vocation and are now supporting school Christian groups as teachers.

Since the early days of the ISCF the main change has been a gradual maturing from a pioneer fellowship of enthusiastic but inexperienced Christian Unions into a highly-respected (and in many places officially encouraged) regional organisation concerned with Christian involvement in every way in school life.

Highlights of Christian Union life are area conferences, leaders' conferences and Summer camps and house parties. It is at these that much of the really effective evangelism is done, though it should be added that any sort of emotional or spiritual pressure on a schoolboy or girl would be quite foreign to the ISCF way of doing things.

Perhaps Jean's story will illustrate how these holidays make their Christian impact felt.

Jean first went to an Inter-School camp at the end of her third year—that is, when she was about fourteen. She had been encouraged to go by her maths mistress, and half a dozen other members of her form were at the camp as well. So far as she could remember she had never exactly dis-believed in God, but religion meant "going to church" and "anything which wasn't actually heathen". This first ISCF camp roused her from her apathy about religion, and after she got back home she read her Bible daily for about a fort-night. But some of her class-mates, a few of whom were becoming uncomfortably aware of the moral demands of the

Christian faith, began to put pressure on her to leave religion well alone. She allowed herself to be discouraged from pursuing the matter any further.

The following year she applied to go to camp again. After all, it had been a good holiday, away from her parents and with girls of her own age. Again her class-mates tried to dissuade her, and she wavered to the extent of attempting to withdraw at the last moment. But when she found that she would probably lose her deposit she decided to ignore their attacks and go.

This time she was much more deeply challenged by the Gospel, as she heard it from the leaders and, very especially, as she saw it in the lives of the Christian girls with whom she shared a dormitory. On the last night of camp she professed conversion; and there was no going back this time, despite repeated scorn and discouragement by her cronies.

Since then she has gone on to university, where she is very active in the Christian Union, and hopes to teach Religious Knowledge in a secondary school.

Not all of those youngsters who come to faith during their schooldays reach a spiritual climax at camp, of course. For many a search which begins at school ends many years later. Such was Margaret's story.

She was in the sixth form of her school before she began to think seriously about Christianity. She could pinpoint the moment in time when interest was first aroused.

They were studying Paul's Letter to the Romans. It was, not surprisingly, pretty hard going and it did not mean much to her until suddenly one verse gripped her attention: "For I do not do the good I want, but the evil I do not want is what I do."

44

"The verse seemed to leap out of the page and hit me," she recalls, "as I realised that this was my experience just as much as it had been Paul's experience in the first place." However, the thought proved extremely disturbing, and, as we do with troublesome ideas, she put it out of her mind. Indeed, in reaction against the first stirrings of faith she deliberately set out to oppose the Gospel. When she started at Teacher Training College she hotly repudiated the faith of a Christian girl in the next room, and did her best to pull her beliefs to pieces, as they argued long into the night.

However, by the next summer she felt that what she really wanted was to find out for herself what was in the Bible, of which she had to date only read snippets. She had not the courage to read it among her friends at college, so she waited for the vacation and then, in her own room, began reading the Old Testament in the morning and the New Testament at night. This went on for some weeks, and gradually the Bible seemed to get a hold on her, and she increased her daily quota from two to four chapters a day, and even slipped upstairs in the middle of the day to continue her reading. Finally there came a night, when she had read the four Gospels and the Bible had very clearly spoken to her, when she knelt by her bed and committed herself wholeheartedly to God through Jesus Christ.

Incidentally, it was not until after this experience that someone introduced her to the Scripture Union way of reading the Bible! Since then she has found even more meaning and relevance in the Scriptures—"the Bible has become a dynamic force, not just a lot of black and white marks on the paper", she says.

It is to help girls like Margaret, serious and intelligent

seekers, that ISCF exists; and it is through Christian girls, and boys, of her calibre that the witness in thousands of schools is carried on.

Of course, there is a lighter side to the subject of school Christian Unions. There is bound to be, when one considers the raw material involved. Boys and girls in the fifth and sixth forms—the ones most concerned with ISCF—are usually a delightful blend of middle-aged solemnity and teen-age exuberance. When you add to this a perfectly serious and genuine interest in the Christian faith, you must expect the occasional lapse into the ludicrous.

One incident from the legends of ISCF—though the story is absolutely true—concerns a grammar school representative who stood up to give a report to a leaders' conference. Adopting a rather pious tone, he related some of the problems the Christian Union in his school had had to face. Very earnestly he reported, "Our last headmaster was very much against our having a Christian Union. But we prayed, and he passed away . . ." The rest of his remarks, after a split second of horrified silence, were lost in a gale of laughter.

An equally embarrassing moment once faced the writer. I was invited to speak to a Christian Union at a girls' school on the subject, "Did Moses write Genesis?" With some misgivings I accepted, and went along prepared to give the qualified affirmative that most people of my views would give. ("Well, let us say that Genesis has Moses' *authority* on it, though it would seem unlikely that he actually wrote every word of it . . .") I had a sneaking suspicion that this was not exactly what the girls wanted, for on my arrival a rather chilly middle-aged lady was propelled towards me by some of the Christian Union members with the breathless introduction, "Sir, this is Miss X. She doesn't believe Moses wrote Genesis!" So I was to be the union's champion against the erring Scripture teacher. I fear I disappointed the girls slightly, and offended the teacher deeply: an impossible situation all round.

On another occasion I was introduced by a rather nervous young chairman to a very undisciplined gathering in these terms: "This is Mr Winter. He taught for four years in a Secondary Modern school, so you lot at the back had better watch out!" I found this the most daunting introduction I have ever been given, and failed dismally (I regret to say) to fulfil the youthful chairman's pathetic confidence in me.

In fact Christian work in schools is both richly rewarding and deeply discouraging. No one should be encouraged to take it on who cannot greet success and failure—those two impostors—if not with a smile, at least with equanimity. In my five years as a teacher I certainly saw both. At one time we had a Christian Union that was the envy of my friends, with as many as a hundred coming to a single meeting, and literally scores of youngsters professing faith in Christ. But, sadly, looking back on it all from ten years or so, most of what was done had little permanency. Undoubtedly largely through my own immaturity and folly, all but a handful of that great crowd of eager young people have long since ceased to compete in the Christian life.

On the other hand, one knows of schools where small groups have achieved astonishing, and apparently permanent, results. A few examples of the way boys and girls have come to mature faith through ISCF and their school

47

Christian Unions will demonstrate both the problems and the possibilities.

John was converted to faith in Christ at an evangelistic meeting, and was fired with the idea of personal witness and forming a Christian Union at school. He soon gathered possible members of such a group, but was unable to get the headmaster's permission. The regional ISCF staff member gave the group a large slice of his time, and the head was persuaded to grant permission for a CU to be formed provided this supervision and advice continued.

Eventually the headmaster changed his attitude, but other problems arose—clashes with times of games practices and opposition by some teachers and pupils. But, with ISCF backing, the group grew, John matured, and the situation changed.

Now, eighteen years later, the Christian Union is strong and well-established, and there are four or five teachers who support it. John, after a spell on the ISCF staff, is now in industry and helps the Fellowship locally.

Another John was converted at an ISCF camp and also returned determined to recruit boys for camp the following year and also start a Christian group in school. Again the headmaster refused permission (no teacher was willing to take responsibility for it), but allowed him to recruit for camp. John took two friends the next year and both were converted. The following year—persistence personified—he took three more, with exactly the same result. Now there was an enthusiastic nucleus, praying for permission to run a Christian Union.

A Christian master was appointed and sponsored a group, which quickly grew and matured. When John left school he became a teacher, and later served on the ISCF staff before returning to teaching again.

A girl—Mary—agreed to attend a marine biology course run by the ISCF. Apart from one subsequent attendance at a CU meeting the course appeared to do rather less for her spiritual state than for her biological knowledge. However, the teacher who encouraged her to attend the course later asked her to help with the catering at an ISCF camp, and Mary accepted. It was at this camp that she was converted to Christ and subsequently she has been a tower of strength to the school (and later college) Christian Union.

Probably enough has been said to support the contention that the Bible speaks today to young people, and that through the Scripture Union, as through many other agencies, a living and abiding word comes to this restless generation. Indeed, one of the really encouraging signs today for Christians is the verifiable fact that more young people than ever before are associated with the different Christian youth movements, with the ISCF, and with university Christian Unions. The Church of Christ can never be written off as a spent force while literally hundreds of thousands of teenagers are prepared openly to identify themselves with its message and "fight manfully under its banner".

Does it all last? We have touched on an answer to this question many times in this chapter, and, of course, the great number of missionaries, ministers and clergy who look back to CSSM beach missions, inland campaigns, holiday camps or house-parties or school Christian Unions as the occasions when God first called them to Himself is in itself the very best answer to the question.

Is it real? To answer that question I cannot do better than

49

D

relate the story of Florence, substantially as told me by her own mother recently.

Florence put her trust in the Lord Jesus Christ at a CSSM beach mission at Frinton in 1955, two days before her twelfth birthday. About two years later she developed cancer of the kidney, and died in hospital after a very big operation before she reached her fifteenth birthday. Just before she died this fourteen-year-old girl wrote to the young lady who had introduced her to Jesus Christ to say that "now there is nothing between me and my Lord". All who knew her at school learned to love her, and many told her parents of her brave witness for Christ. Her own mother wrote, "Her life after her conversion was truly transformed —she was a 'new creature' in Christ Jesus."

Is *that* sort of faith real? To ask the question is an impertinence. If the good news of Christ can enable a mere child of fourteen to face pain and death like that, then it is good news indeed.

CHAPTER 3

For Unlikely People

Jim was the sort of boy you could not help liking. One of the masters in the approved school to which he was regularly committed by the juvenile court called him a "lovable rogue". Since he was eleven he had been in and out of approved schools. While he was in, he got on well, but the moment he returned home something went wrong.

Not that this was surprising. Jim's father had left them soon after his younger sister was born and had never been seen nor heard of since. Mother lived with the children in an old Nissen hut, in filthy and insanitary conditions.

When Jim came to the school there was one part of the day which he found very trying. This was the half-hour when the boys were permitted to lie on their beds and read. He found it difficult to while away this half-hour—reading was not his strong point and ordinary books left him cold.

Possibly out of sheer boredom he asked the Scripture Union staff member who visits the approved school in his area for a copy of the Bible. What is more, with the aid of the *Invitation to Live* introductory reading notes, he actually began to read it. He did not find it easy, it was often heavy going for him, but with commendable tenacity he kept at it and, unknown to anybody, the personality of Jesus Christ began to fascinate him.

As the time came for Jim to leave once again the question arose as to where he should stay. Actually he agreed to live in lodgings away from his old, unhelpful surroundings, but, just before he was due to go, he asked for an interview and made what was on all counts a remarkable statement.

"Sir," he said, "I am most grateful for all that has been done in trying to get me away from my home and those surroundings, but, sir, I want you to know that life for me is different now. Since reading the Bible I see things differently. I'm going back home. I'm going to help my mother and my sister and I'm going to make our lives really worth while."

Jim was as good as his word. He returned home, and transformed that Nissen hut from a squalid shack into a clean, neat dwelling. He told his mother and sister what he had read in the Bible, and together they started going to church regularly on Sundays, and each night they would sit together for a time and read and try to understand the Bible. The transformation is generally regarded by those who know Jim best as bordering on the miraculous. Others, who know God, would consider that it crosses the border.

Jim's story is a good introduction to the work of the two Scripture Union staff members who spend their time visiting Borstals and approved schools, getting to know the boys and girls and setting out to provide them with spiritual counsel and pastoral care. It is slow, often unrewarding work, and few of the youngsters in the schools are anything but suspicious on first contact with the "Bible punchers". Yet no area of the SU's work has produced such startling evidence of the power of God's living and abiding word as this one.

Joe, for example, was a hard case: a beautiful athlete, standing over six feet tall, a semi-coloured lad of massive proportions but superb physique. He was rough and tough, violent and cynical. He came to the home after a series of extremely serious offences, but nothing seemed to shake his massive indifference. "I'm too big to read the Bible. I'm too *tired* to worry about those things." All through prayers each evening he would sit, smiling sarcastically, apparently utterly impermeable.

So it was a considerable surprise when he came up one night and asked if he could borrow a Bible as he wanted to read it "for himself". Thereafter, night by night, during the quiet half-hour at the close of the day, big Joe could be seen poring over the Bible. He, too, was using the *Invitation to Live* readings and, unknown to anybody, the Word of God was making its own deep impression on this "hard case".

Before he was discharged Joe had put his trust in Jesus Christ, and he went home a changed young man. His life's story, however, is by no means finished yet, for Joe— that is not his real name, of course—is now the member of a famous athletic club and recently won a place in the England athletic team.

Ken was a completely different case. He had a good home—his father was a sergeant in the Army—and was at the local grammar school. But when he was fifteen tragedy struck. His mother died suddenly and the home was broken up and Ken was put in the care of relatives. From the start he failed to adjust himself to this new home, there may well have been faults on both sides, and things went from bad to worse.

There was a temporary improvement when he left school (before taking his GCE) and got a job in the post office. But he began to get into difficulties again, spent money that was not his own and was eventually caught embezzling money from the bank. The court committed him to a probation home, and he was sent to one where the warden was a Christian man.

At his initial interview things did not look too promising. After the practical details had been sorted out, Ken pushed back his chair and faced the warden aggressively across the table.

"They tell me you're a Bible puncher," he said. "I want you to know that I don't believe in God and I don't believe the Bible either."

"All right, Ken," the man replied, "All right. Let's just try living together and see what comes of it in the future, shall we?"

For the next few months Ken lived in the home with thirty other fellows, no worse and no better than most of them. During this time, with encouragement, he took and passed two more subjects in GCE, and then arrangements were made for him to go to the local technical college, where he got more passes both at "O" and "A" level.

One Saturday evening Ken came and knocked at the office door and asked if he could have a chat. The warden asked him in and after some pleasantries Ken suddenly said, "Sir, could you either give me or loan me a Bible? I'd like to read it."

He departed clutching a brand new Bible (kindly

provided for the home by the Scripture Gift Mission) and several times over the next few weeks he was discovered in unlikely places reading it. It was obvious that the book and its message fascinated him.

Then one Sunday evening after the service Ken asked for another private interview, and this time he wanted not a book but a Person, Jesus Christ. He received Him, having met Him, in his own words, "just through reading the Bible".

Ken's story, like Joe's, is incomplete. He is at university reading sociology, and hopes one day to be a probation officer, helping boys in trouble.

That is one of the most impressive things about this Christian work amongst young people who have got into trouble—that the change after they meet with Christ is so dramatic and complete, and there is often a totally new conception of service and care for others. For Jim, it was a new concern for his home, his mother and sister. For Ken, a new concern for boys like himself. For David, a fourteen year old in an approved school, it became his fellow-pupils and the local village.

David was in a home where the house parents were both Christians, and, like so many of these allegedly "tough" lads, when he was given a Bible he began to read it. As he did, he came face to face with the Person of Jesus Christ, and soon put his trust in Him. Later, when they saw the difference this made in David's life, two of his closest friends also turned to Christ.

The influence of these three boys on the school was tremendous. The other boys and the staff were staggered at the difference their conversions had made to them. The

Scripture Union worker was from then on warmly welcomed and he found staff and boys eager to find out what it was all about. Regularly, week by week, forty out of the ninety boys in the school met voluntarily for Bible reading and study.

When David and his friends were given leave to visit the local village they decided that what had been such a help to them could also be a help to the villagers. They thought the church was the right place to begin, so they went up to the rectory and boldly knocked on the door. The elderly incumbent was surprised to see three lads from the approved school on his doorstep.

"Do you have a Bible study we could come to here, sir?" they asked politely.

The old rector shook his head. "No, no—and the people never ask for one."

"Well," the boys came back, "Couldn't you start one?" And they went on to tell him what the Bible had done for them.

The rector was duly impressed and promised to think about it. In fact, he did more. He approached the Methodist minister in the next village, and between them they started a Bible study meeting for their villages. The boys went along, of course, to learn—and to contribute a great deal, too. The rector was so impressed with them, and by their concern to help others, that he took them with him on visits to a mental hospital and an old people's home in the parish, where the boys were able to read the Bible and tell the patients what it meant to them.

So the wheel turns full circle. The boys were anti-social, misfits, maladjusted; a potentially dangerous influence in the community. So society put them in an approved school. But there they learned an answer to their needs which seems to escape many social workers and reformers, and eventually became outstandingly helpful and committed members of the very society that had disciplined them. There must be a moral there, somewhere.

Of course, it would be quite irresponsible to claim that all that is needed to help maladjusted and anti-social teenagers is to "preach the Gospel" to them. And it would be misleading to give the impression that every juvenile delinquent is willing and waiting to respond to the Gospel when he hears it. These stories are exceptional, needless to say. Most of the time Christian work amongst these boys and girls (just like any work amongst them) is a question of patience, unjudging friendship and love, understanding and scrupulous fairness. But these stories do show that the Bible has a relevance and realism to youngsters who, often through unhappy home life or broken marriages, are outwardly hard, cynical or scornful.

Perhaps of all the stories connected with Scripture Union work amongst teenagers in trouble the most remarkable is Dorothy's. This is partly because of the depths to which she had sunk, and partly because of the amazing way she was lifted out of them.

Unlike most of the boys we have described, Dorothy came from a good and affluent home. Her parents were kind to her, and in many ways she was a particularly well favoured young girl. Yet at only fourteen she announced that grammar school was not the place for her, and at the first legal opportunity she left.

She began to spend more and more time on the streets of

the town, became sexually experienced and then promiscuous. At first secretly, but later more or less openly, she took to the life of a common prostitute. Her parents were powerless to help her or stop her.

The next stage, as so often with girls in her situation, was drug-taking. As sexual excitement palls through mis-use, and the deep loneliness of the unattached sweeps in, only drugs, with their bogus benevolence, seem able to help. Dorothy started by smoking reefers, got herself addicted, and ended up a "main line" drug taker—that is to say, she injected the drugs straight into her blood-stream intravenously: the last and most desperate stage of addiction. Drugs cost money—more money than she could earn on the streets in her present condition.

So the sadly familiar progression continued: from promiscuity to drugs, from drugs to petty theft—and, almost inevitably, from petty theft to court and from court to Borstal. At just nineteen, Dorothy was a physical, social and moral wreck. She looked twice her age, could not survive without regular drugs, and was almost incapable of lucid reasoning. In Borstal she was given medical and psychiatric help, and there was some improvement; but when she was released she went back to her life of soliciting and drug taking. Again when money ran short she took to petty thieving, and again she was caught and eventually sent back to Borstal. For the second time the normal medical treatment for an addict—the very slow and very painful process known as "withdrawal"—was begun.

It was at this desperate juncture in her life that she met the Scripture Union worker. She asked him for a Bible—apparently insincerely—and was given one, together with the inevitable copy of *Invitation to Live*. Sarcastically she commented, "Just what I've been looking for!"

In fact, she never spoke a truer word. With the help of the notes she read right through John's Gospel. Then she read it through again—and again, sixteen times in all, she later claimed, until Jesus Christ became intensely real to her through its pages.

One night soon after this, at turned midnight, the other girls in her dormitory were surprised to see Dorothy climb out of bed, tears streaming down her face, and kneel down, flinging her face on to the bed clothes, sobbing uncontrollably. They were even more surprised to hear her pray between the sobs: "God—if there is a God, and if this Jesus I've been reading about in the Bible is real and alive—then let me meet Him, here, now." There was a moment of utter silence, and then Dorothy scrambled back into bed and, apparently, to sleep.

Every morning Dorothy had to go and see the doctor to be given her carefully controlled dosage of drug, as part of the withdrawal process. The doctor thought she looked a bit brighter than usual, and said so.

"Yes, doctor," she agreed, "I do feel much better this morning. And I shan't be needing any of your drugs any more."

"No more drugs? Why is that?"

"Well sir, last night I met Jesus Christ—you know, the man in the Bible."

The doctor looked at her wide-eyed, and sent for the psychiatrist. Together they extracted the full story from her, of her reading of the New Testament, her dawning awareness of the reality of Jesus Christ, and her tortured prayer of the previous night. When they had done this they were so astonished that they sent for the Governor, and Dorothy was made to repeat her story to him. Between the three of them they could not explain what had happened, but gave Dorothy five days to prove to their satisfaction that she would not be needing any more drugs.

The five days passed, and still Dorothy had not asked for any drugs. The days lengthened into months, and it became clear to everybody that what Dorothy had claimed was completely true: the living Christ had delivered this poor, desperate, latter-day Magdalene from the most bitter depths of depravity.

Eventually she left the Borstal institution, and the Scripture Union worker was able to find her a home with a Christian couple, far away from her old surroundings and temptations. She found a good, steady job, and made many friends in the local church where she worships and witnesses. She is by any standards a remarkable testimony to the grace of God and the living word which brings new life to the dead.

The remarkably consistent thing about these stories of boys and girls in approved school and Borstals is the impact of Jesus Christ Himself, as found in the pages of the New Testament. Perhaps it is that these youngsters see in Him all that they cannot find in themselves. Perhaps it is the sheer contrast of light and darkness, between confused, fallen youth and God's "proper Man". Perhaps it is the compassion and yet firmness, the "grace and truth" of His character. Whatever the reason, it is a remarkable fact that cynical and tough young men and women, who find nothing much to attract them in religion or the Church, find utter reality and relevance in Him.

It is this that is important about these stories, in a wider context. In themselves they are uniquely personal testimonies, fairly far removed from the situations most people know, exceptional in the true meaning of the word. But at a deeper level they are of universal relevance, for they demonstrate what is the heart of the Christian Gospel: that Jesus Christ came not for the healthy, but for the sick; not for the righteous (whatever that may mean), but for "sinners". The saying is sure: "Christ Jesus came into the world to save sinners". Wherever there is sin, and wherever there are sinners, the good news of Christ is relevant: and that is everywhere.

For "this Man"—and, please God, those who follow Him "*this* Man receives sinners".

CHAPTER 4

For People with Problems

They had been expecting it for some time, but it was still a difficult thing to accept.

"You see, Mrs Oldcastle," the child psychiatrist had said, "your little daughter will never make real progress while she stays at home. You know that she is seriously backward, mentally handicapped compared with other children—compared with *your* other children, for example. She is not insane, or anything like that, but she does need special care and expert teaching—and you couldn't possibly find the time to give it to her, even if you knew how to. In any case, your other children would suffer if you attempted it.

"Now this will not be an easy decision for you, but I hope you and your husband will agree to her entering a special boarding school. If you decide to let her go, you will have to spend several weeks carefully preparing her for this big change in her life—we shall tell you what to do and help you all we can."

Mr and Mrs Oldcastle talked it over at length and, because they were both committed Christians, they prayed about it, too. Though they dearly loved their backward little daughter, they knew in their heart of hearts that it would be right to let her go away to school, and signed the necessary papers.

Then began the slow process of preparing the little girl for the transition. The idea had to be sown in her mind, and made to sound very attractive, and the other children had to be shown how to co-operate by saying just the right things and helping their little sister, in her simple way, to come to terms with the move which she only vaguely understood.

It was all over very quickly, and quite painlessly for the child. The car came for her, she kissed them all good-bye, and as the car drove off she was wreathed in smiles at the thought of the unexpected ride. The Oldcastle family went indoors, mother and father very relieved that there had been no complications. It was not until some time later—on the following Saturday, to be precise—that the full significance of what had happened dawned on them, and especially on mother.

"We suddenly realised how much we missed her," she recalls. "So much time had been spent preparing her for this step in her life that no thought had been given to preparing the rest of the family for the gap that would be left in our lives. I had a peculiar, lost kind of feeling, and on that Saturday morning my pent up feelings just flowed out in many tears."

Has the Bible, the "living, abiding word", anything to say to people in that sort of situation? The next morning gave the answer. As usual mother turned to the Scripture Union passage for the day and began to read: "Thus saith the Lord, A voice was heard in Ramah, lamentation and bitter weeping; Rachel weeping for her children refused to be comforted for her children, because they were not. Thus said the Lord, Refrain thy voice from weeping, and thine eyes from tears: for thy work shall be rewarded, saith the Lord; and they shall come again from the land of the enemy" (Jeremiah 31: 15, 16).

"It was as though the Lord Himself spoke to me," says Mrs Oldcastle, "and I wept no more. In the evening our other little girl burst into tears before going to bed—she was missing her sister—and I was able to comfort her as I had been comforted."

It is possible to dismiss a story like that as coincidence, though the frequency of this sort of experience argues strongly against it. In any case, the important thing is that the Word of God *did* bring comfort and help, precisely when it was needed and in the most immediate and practical way. This is the mark of life: adaptability. The same living book which in earlier chapters we have seen bringing unbelievers and seekers to faith in Christ is now seen bringing comfort, strength and guidance to mature Christian believers.

So we come to what is in fact a basic ministry of the Scripture Union—encouraging and helping Christians to read their Bibles regularly, believingly and expectantly.

There have always been Christians who have rebelled at regular, consistent Bible study. Some have preferred the random reading, hoping that by jumping from place to place they would find a "blessed thought" for the day. Some have been content to read and re-read a few favourite passages, generally of sentimental or aesthetic appeal. Some have only read the Bible when they have felt like it.

All of these approaches to the Bible show a fundamental misconception of its nature.

To those who jump from place to place in search of "blessed thoughts" one has to say that the Bible is not a collection of texts, but a book with a coherent theme and a message which is only fully conveyed by the whole. Verses torn from their context to provide "instant guidance" or "instant uplift" are mutilated messengers of the truth. God has given in the Bible a total revelation which can only be valued properly and applied rightly if each part is seen in relation to the whole.

The Bible is not magic, and we do it no honour to treat it like one of those "What the Stars Foretell" columns in the daily papers. God may well give a special message to a young and uninstructed Christian through a "random" reading, but the Bible's deepest truths and purest wisdom are for those who are prepared to dig deep for them. He spoke to the Oldcastles through their regular, daily reading. He could not have spoken more clearly if they had opened the Bible at random fifty times over.

To those who read and re-read favourite passages one has to point out that the Bible is not primarily an anthology of great literature but a record of God's dealings with men. By concentrating on favourite passages we isolate certain aspects of truth which appeal to us, and shut our minds to other truths which we may find unpalatable. So a man who never moves far beyond the twenty-third psalm and the Sermon on the Mount may well know of the kindness of God, but not His severity; and of the unattainable moral standards set by Christ, but not of His ransom to pay the price of our failure to reach them. Much of the error, confusion and

65

prejudice in the Church today can be traced to the fact that comparatively few church-goers know the *whole* of the Bible's message.

To those who only read the Bible when the mood strikes them one has to warn that the very moments when we need it most are often the very moments when we least feel like reading it.

Each of these erroneous approaches to the Bible is avoided by the Scripture Union method of regular, systematic, daily reading, covering virtually the whole Bible over a period of years. The stories in this chapter, telling of ways in which God has used those readings to speak to people's deep personal needs are, therefore, testimonies not to the Bible's "magical" properties, but to its living quality of speaking, to those who know it, love it and *use it rightly*, with unique clarity and aptness.

Mr F.C. is a good example of this. He has read the SU's *Daily Bread* portions, with occasional interruptions, for about thirty years, so he is no addict of random reading. In February 1953, he had to enter hospital for a very serious operation which was to last several hours.

"Before going down to the operating theatre," he relates, "I read as usual the Scripture Union portion for the day, and as I finished the nurse arrived to give me the pre-medication injection which is popularly but erroneously said to put you to sleep before arriving in the theatre for anaesthetic. In spite of a natural anxiety I did doze off in confidence and the note in my Bible reminds me that the passage that day was Psalm 4, including, of course, verse 8 which reads, 'I will both lay me down in peace, and sleep: for thou, Lord, only makest me dwell in safety'."

A very similar experience is related by a lady who was greatly encouraged by the Scripture Union's choice of Joshua 1: 9 on the morning of her major operation—"Be not afraid . . . the Lord thy God is with thee withersoever thou goest."

A lady in Bristol tells how the Scripture Union reading for one particular day spoke to all her family.

They had been going through a very difficult time, with a major problem hanging over the household. The trouble was being caused by malicious enemies, and seemed beyond solution. On a Thursday morning the reading was Psalm 37: 1–20—"Fret not yourself because of the wicked, be not envious of wrong-doers. . . Commit your way to the Lord; trust in Him, and he will act. He will bring forth your vindication as the light, and your right as the noonday . . . Refrain from anger, and forsake wrath! Fret not yourself; it tends only to evil. . . Better is a little that the righteous has than the abundance of many wicked." It was like a direct message from God.

That evening mother was discussing this remarkably apt reading with her husband and grandmother. They read it through again, together. Then the son came in from evening classes and his first words were, "What about the SU for yesterday? Did you think it applied to me?" On reflection, it certainly did.

Then, to make it complete, the next day they had a letter from their married daughter, who said, "Didn't you think the SU portion was lovely for Wednesday – and how it fitted my experience just now!" Again, on reflection, it did indeed exactly speak to her circumstances. So, in two days, and without any "collusion", the Bible gave three "personal messages" to one family.

This sort of reward comes to those who look for it, just as prayer is a more effective weapon on the lips of the one who often speaks to God. To read expectantly is another mark of Christian maturity—that is to say, expecting that God will speak, looking for His personal messages as well as His general proclamations.

One SU reader in London kept a note over a period of a few months of distinct "personal" messages that her regular daily Bible reading brought her.

They included three distinct instances of advice to her on her personal relationships at home and at work, and with Christians and non-Christians:

"Do not return evil for evil or reviling for reviling; but on the contrary bless, for to this you have been called, that you may obtain a blessing" (1 Peter 3: 9).

"Let us have no self-conceit, no provoking of one another, no envy of one another. . . For if one thinks he is something, when he is nothing, he deceives himself" (Galatians 5: 26, 6: 3).

"And we exhort you, brethren, admonish the idle, encourage the faint-hearted, help the weak, be patient with them all" (1 Thessalonians 5: 14).

Then there was a promise of God's guidance for her at the beginning of a new year which might bring change and uncertainty:

"I will instruct you and teach you the way you should go; I will counsel you with my eye upon you" (Psalm 32: 8).

There was a reminder, when national and international

affairs caused anxiety and concern, of God's steadfast love for all men and every nation and His sovereign power in their affairs: "The Lord brings the counsel of the nations to naught; he frustrates the plans of the peoples. . . A king is not saved by his great army; a warrior is not delivered by his great strength. . . Our soul waits for the Lord; he is our help and shield" (Psalm 33: 10, 16, 20). "He shall judge between many peoples, and shall decide for strong nations afar off; and they shall beat their swords into ploughshares, and their spears into pruning hooks; nation shall not lift up sword against nation, neither shall they learn war any more" (Micah 4: 3).

And there was a warning when she took an unsympathetic attitude to a colleague who was taken ill, apparently because of a lack of common sense:

"But you should not have gloated over the day of your brother in his misfortune . . ." (Obadiah 12).

Now all of these quotations are statements of general truth, applicable at all times, or else revelations of God's character and Person, which do not alter. So it is manifestly fitting to apply them to one's personal situation and circumstances. But how many readers of the Bible would think to do so? It is a useful exercise to read those passages of Scripture carefully, and try to reconstruct the personal situation which made them seem so relevant to the reader. Those who read the Bible and only see their schemes of salvation, doctrines, and textual problems are missing the wood for the trees. The Bible speaks to *people*. It is the reader who turns to it expecting to find help, correction, advice or warning who finds it there. After all, that is just what the Scriptures claim they are intended to do: they are "profitable for teaching, for reproof, for correction, and for training in righteousness, that the *man of God* may be complete . . ."

However, it would be wrong to suggest that the Bible never speaks to those in need who are not regular readers of it. God, in Peter's memorable phrase, "has no favourites". The story of Mrs Trent will help to illustrate this.

She was a harrassed mother of three, with a good home and happy family life, but a bit bored with living in a remote part of the country. She was also a discontented and vaguely dissatisfied person, longing for something to give her life meaning.

One day her little son Michael, who was four, came running in with his sisters (seven and eight years old) and asked if they could all go to "Sunday school" that evening. She discovered that he meant a special children's meeting that had been arranged in a local chapel by the Scripture Union evangelist.

Later that evening, after the meeting, Micky burst into the room and announced breathlessly, "1 John 4: 8, God is love". For some reason the simple text stuck in her mind, and after the children were in bed Mrs Trent found a Bible in the cupboard and looked it up. Not finding it in John 4: 8, which was something about a Samaritan woman, she assumed he had got the reference wrong and began to search for the verse all through John's Gospel—without finding it, needless to say.

Disturbed more than she was prepared to admit by those three simple words, and put out by her inability to find them in the Bible, she asked Micky for the reference again at breakfast. She got the same answer, "1 John 4: 8, God is love". Still the important first digit failed to register, and she reluctantly gave up the search.

However, the evangelist made a surprise call at her home that morning, and almost her first words to him were, "Where do I find 1 John 4: 8 in the Bible?" He turned her to the first Epistle of John, and for the first time in her life she read the words for herself: "He who does not love does not know God; for God is love". The same week she went to the mission meetings and received Jesus Christ as her Saviour.

But that is not the end of the story. There was a much deeper significance in the underlining of the phrase "God is love" than any of those involved could possibly have known at the time. For within six months Michael, the innocent messenger who brought the light of God into his home through just three words of Scripture, was taken ill and died. Only then—but how deeply, then—did Mrs Trent fully appreciate the loving care of God, who had prepared her for this devastating blow and assured her before it happened that His love for her, for her little son, and for the whole family, was as fixed and steadfast as His own nature.

The Psalmist said that God's Word was a lamp to his feet and a light to his path: that is, general illumination of the broad outline of the way through life, and light on each particular step of the way. So we may look to the Bible for help in the major decisions of life and in the details of our daily activities.

A major decision facing a mature Christian woman concerned her possible marriage to a divorced man whose first wife was still alive. For a long time she went backwards and forwards over the arguments, took advice which often proved inconclusive, and prayed about it frequently.

However, it was not until she came to Romans 7: 1–12 in her Scripture Union readings that she had a clear lead on the subject. The notes on the passage, which is not, of course, primarily concerned with marriage and divorce, read: "These verses, though quoted for another purpose, emphasise the Christian teaching about marriage as a life-long union, broken only by death, when re-marriage (verse 3b) is right and honourable." There seemed nothing more to be said!

A decision of less permanent significance, but of considerable importance at the time, faced a Scripture Union reader in Norfolk. After only five months in her first job, with a firm of solicitors, she came home one evening to find that her mother had arranged an interview for her with another firm. The young woman's first reaction was to refuse to go, but she felt she ought at least to pray about it before dismissing the idea as unthinkable. In the event, she went for the interview and was offered the job, but was still undecided, and had to make her decision by nine o'clock the following morning.

Weighing up the advantages and disadvantages, she felt more and more drawn to the new job, and then took what was for her an unusual step: she asked God to confirm this impression before "zero hour" the next morning. The passage chosen by the Scripture Union the next morning spoke with impressive simplicity, so far as she was concerned: "Go, do all that is in thine heart, for the Lord is with thee!" For the record, later events amply proved that this was the right decision to have made.

"Need" is not always a sudden thing facing us and then passed. For some people it is a lifelong experience. It is for Miss Gill, who, at about the same time as she committed her life to Jesus Christ in a Caravan Mission meeting in her village, fell victim to a disease which subsequently incapacitated her and left her more or less chair-bound for life. This happened when she was twelve, and much of the rest of her youth was spent in and out of hospital. Her spiritual life suffered, but at eighteen God spoke to her very clearly at a meeting in a local chapel, confirming the experience she had had as a child, and she was baptised. This was a great test for her, as she felt she should be baptised by immersion and obviously this would be difficult for her. In fact, she says, "it proved not to be an ordeal at all, but a truly wonderful experience".

From that point on in her life she has been claiming God's promise to Paul, that "my grace is sufficient for you, for my power is made perfect in weakness". Although the doctors said that by now she would be quite helpless, she is in fact still able to earn her own living, drive an invalid car, get to church on Sunday mornings and generally lead a very full life.

"So sure am I," she writes, "that in my weakness I have received an over-abundant share of His grace, that I would not be healed of my physical infirmity, even if I could be, if by so doing I would lessen even a little the wonderful fellowship and friendship that He has given me in my weakness."

God speaks to people in their need, and gives grace to people in their weakness. Human agencies like the Scripture reading notes or the Caravan Mission may be used by Him to meet those needs and minister to those weaknesses, but let us be very clear that the grace is His, and His alone.

It would be quite wrong to have a book about the Bible and succeed in giving the impression that it is only concerned with the problems and needs of individuals. There is always a danger, in relating individual testimonies, of giving the impression that Christianity, the Gospel and the message of the Bible have nothing to say to "man in society". Our own personal salvation is vitally important, of course: there can be no growth, no service, no "fruits of the Spirit" without rebirth. Dead men not only tell no tales, they do no deeds. But God has always spoken to nations, communities and societies as well. The Bible's message is relevant both to my individual, daily needs and to the problems and needs of the society of which I am a member.

Now it must be conceded that the Scripture Union, like many another great evangelical institution of the last century, did concentrate for many years on the cultivation of individual piety. Always, of course, there was a strong moral note in its teaching, but it steered clear of directly applying the passages read to current moral and social problems.

However, in recent years the SU has been something of a pioneer group amongst Evangelicals in this sphere. Urged on by a number of very able younger men on its Council and staff, it has in the post-war years been progressively less reticent about relating the Bible's teaching to topical problems. It is not at all unusual to find a note on a daily Bible reading which applies a general biblical truth to some twentieth century problem like the care of the aged, the needs of underdeveloped countries, or the evils of racial prejudice.

The trend is even more marked in other fields of the work. The Inter-School Christian Fellowship, through the magazine *Viewpoint* (and its predecessor, *Pilgrim*) or its rallies and conferences, has publicly come to grips with such twentieth century problems as nuclear disarmament, racial relationships, divorce and industrial disputes, the "new morality", a Christian approach to politics, and so on. Indeed, so uninhibited has the discussion been on some areas of morality that older Christians eaves-dropping at ISCF functions have been known to be more than a little shocked. And a book by J. B. Donovan, *Inside Story*, which the SU published a couple of years ago, was publicly denounced by some older Christians on the ground that it was thinly-disguised pornography. In fact it was a superbly positive book on sex, showing a healthy delight in God's gift of sexuality and giving wise and warm-hearted counsel to its readers. It was universally praised by the Christian press of all shades of opinion, but earned the Scripture Union a few black marks in other quarters. It is not just in words, either, that this has happened. The ISCF has run work parties and work camps in Notting Hill on re-housing schemes.

Happily the signs are that the movement will continue to take its stand on an approach to Bible reading which is personal but not narrowly individualistic, and devotional but not self-centred. It will continue to relate the truths of God and the love and grace of Christ to every aspect of daily life and every area of society.

CHAPTER 5

For Enlisted People

Jean became clear that she was a Christian at half-past ten on a Friday night. For some years she had attended church, and this was not a case of sudden conversion, but rather a dawning realisation that God loved her and wanted her to belong to Him. Yet the moment when this tremendous fact crystallised in her mind was a real turning point. For the first time ever she felt able to join in the communion service the following Sunday, and her minister, whom she had told of her experience, gave her a copy of the Scripture Union book *The Way*, by Godfrey Robinson and Stephen Winward. An elder at the church, who had first brought her along several years before, gave her a Bible the same day, so she felt well equipped to face her first Monday morning as a committed Christian.

She remembers waking up the next morning to the thought that she was now a Christian and that God would be with her all day at work—an advertising agency for which she had no great enthusiasm. It was a tremendous moment: Monday mornings were usually short-tempered, grey and depressing. Armed with her copy of *The Way*, she sallied forth to work.

She went out to lunch alone, and over her something and chips began to read.

76

"I was told to read my Bible every day," she recalls, "pray every day, control my tongue and read the Scripture Union notes (or something like that—it escapes me now!). *None of these things had occurred to me.* Reading that book on the second day of my Christian experience set me on the path and told me how to use the weapons at my disposal, and to start fighting the great fight of faith."

Jean's story, quite ordinary in its way, introduces another aspect of the ministry of the Scripture Union—to help Christians grow to spiritual maturity and go on to Christian service. This is, of course, a Bible ministry; for it is the word of God that "builds us up", as Paul told the Ephesian elders, and the word of God that calls us and commissions us for Christian service, as happened to John the Baptist in the wilderness. It is the work of Scripture Union to be a means for that living word to reach God's people, whether directly through Bible reading, or indirectly through its books and magazines, its evangelists and staff workers and holiday activities. It is only one among many such means, all of them in turn part of Christ's Church, the Body in which we "grow up in every way into Him who is the Head". In other words, this is a ministry of the Bible within the Church.

This can be seen in the story of George, a country boy in Norfolk who is now a Free Church minister in Yorkshire. He was, in his own words, "the very ill-educated son of a farm-worker" who trusted Christ during a CMVC mission in his village. Soon after he wrote to the evangelist saying that he wanted to do well at school, gain a scholarship, go to college, take a degree and enter the ministry. Anything more unlikely, humanly speaking, it would be hard to imagine.

"Entirely due to the Lord's help"—his own words again—he went to grammar school. Conversion seemed to have unlocked some hitherto closed doors in his mind, for he did well at school. Every year he camped at Scripture Union camps, where he was eager to learn the Christian faith and master the Bible's message.

Eventually he went to college and—as he had said he wanted to do as a ten-year-old—he got a BD degree and was ordained in 1954. Part of his work now is training Sunday school teachers and local preachers, and he says, "I consider that the Lord has particularly called me to help those who have not had the advantage of a good education, and yet who feel the call to preach or teach, and feel sure that this is why He called someone from a village background who knew something of the situation." He adds, "The way in which God brought me first to Christ and then into His service has been nothing but a long story of grace from beginning to end."

The phenomenon of a hitherto dull and apparently unintelligent person suddenly making great intellectual strides after conversion is not at all uncommon—which suggests that the frequent complaint that an evangelical conversion tends to stifle the intellect and narrow the mind is far from the truth. A school-teacher at a secondary modern school in Wales tells of a boy who was almost backward and virtually illiterate, who, after his conversion, quickly learned to read and in other ways changed enormously.

In these two cases it was conversion itself which set in train events leading on to Christian growth and service. Very often, of course, the Bible speaks to people who have been Christians for many years—possibly, all their lives—to call them to some new step of faith or service.

Mrs Irene Clegg (for once that is a real name) was converted in 1960 and almost at once was introduced to the Scripture Union daily notes and became a regular reader of the Bible. This in itself, she says, helped her spiritual progress enormously. A country-woman herself, she saw that the printed word could have a tremendous influence in the lives of people cut off from the social life of towns and villages, in the remoter rural areas. With the encouragement of the Secretary of the Farmers' Christian Postal Service, which mails Christian literature to remote farmsteads up and down Britain, she began a "Sunday school by post" to children who were unable to get to ordinary Sunday schools.

Finding the children, and then enrolling them, is no easy task. Yet since 1962, when it began, over 500 children in 237 homes have joined the "Sunday school by post", and 42 adults from those same families have become regular Scripture Union readers. Mrs Clegg uses the SU Sunday school material, *Adventurers*, *Friends of God* and *Pilot* leaflets, and sends the SU paper *Homes and Parents* to the parents of the children.

A similar story, though in a very different field, is that of Mrs Hooker. She, too, lives on a very isolated farm in Devon, in a thirteen-roomed rambling farmhouse. Although busy enough, with four children to bring up, she was very conscious that she had no opportunity for Christian service. Although she longed to serve God, it was hard to see how, in her circumstances, this could be done—beyond, of course, her very important "Christian service" as a wife and mother.

However, one day she saw an advertisement in a local

paper asking for a home for foster children. The idea seemed crazy, with four children of her own, but after a good deal of prayer and thought, and careful scrutiny by the welfare officials, she was accepted as a foster parent and over a period had two or three children to foster temporarily, while their own families, for one reason or another, were unable to cope with them. This she found a really satisfying avenue of service.

But then followed a period when no children were sent to her, and Mrs Hooker began to wonder whether she ought not to volunteer for the more difficult, but more important, role of a permanent foster mother to one child. Previously she had rejected this idea, as she had not wanted to become so deeply involved.

Yet the idea persisted. She felt it right to pursue the question at least as far as being approved by a children's welfare officer. The result was that she found herself being faced with a definite proposition, to foster on a more or less permanent basis a little eighteen-month-old boy.

Now she had to reach a decision. Could she cope? Would her own family suffer? Would she let down this little one who was to be entrusted to her care? She prayed, and friends prayed for her.

On Monday, January 18th, 1965, the SU passage was Genesis 11: 27–32, and 12: 1–9—God's call to Abram. The notes referred her to Hebrews 11: 8. To Mrs Hooker, in an unmistakable way, Abram's call was her call: "By faith Abraham obeyed when he was called . . . and he went out, not knowing where he was to go." She made up her mind to accept the child. Within a few hours the welfare officer had called, quite unexpectedly, to ask for her decision.

A year later Mrs Hooker could look back and see how right that decision was. The little boy is a much-loved and happy member of the family—"he is a ray of sunshine for us all", she says. There were difficulties, "the early days weren't easy," but "I have learned to rely more deeply on the Lord and to test the value of the great promises."

So the Scripture Union, or rather the Word of God through the agency of the Scripture Union, has had a vital role in calling a village boy into the ministry, a housewife to start a postal Sunday school for farm children and a busy mother to foster a little boy without a home. These are just three examples—and unspectacular ones have been chosen quite deliberately—of the way God uses the Scriptures to call His people to growth and service. They could be multiplied endlessly, not only relating to service in Britain, but also "to the ends of the earth".

It was the Scripture Union reading, for example, that called Margery Hancock to missionary service with the Christian Literature Crusade in Japan. "One morning I was reading the SU portion when God spoke to me personally through these words, 'Let thine eyes be on the field that they do reap, and go thou after them'" (Ruth 2: 9). So for her a simple piece of advice to Ruth from a wealthy farmer on the best way to glean after his reapers became a call to follow those who were already "harvesting" for God in the Far East. This, as we have seen before, is the hallmark of a living word: it still speaks, it is always contemporary.

Scripture Union proved a help in an even more direct and practical way to a young airman serving in the Middle East trouble spot, the Yemen. Just before his posting overseas he visited the SU stand at the Devon Show, Exeter. He asked for the *Daily Bread* notes to be sent to him.

Later he wrote from the Yemeni border: "I would like to take the opportunity of thanking you for the pleasure I, and the lads of my squadron, receive from these small books. We rarely see anyone, save for the odd camel train in the distance. *Daily Bread* notes serve as a calendar, prayer-book and ideas for the short talks I give to the lads each Sunday (we don't have a padre of our own). These lads are as hard as nails, but as one of them said, 'God is nearer to me now than ever before, because someone of my own age has explained it in my language'."

Japan, the Yemen: God has used different aspects of the SU's work to call men and women to serve him all over the world. A "follow-up" list of workers at a CSSM beach mission shows that from it, "directly or indirectly", men and women have gone to serve God in Nigeria (seven) Ghana (three), Uganda (two), Zambia, Pakistan, Morocco, the Philippines, Ethiopia and Persia.

The beach mission in question is itself a testimony to the direct call of God. The two people who subsequently became its leaders were sitting one sunny Summer day on the beach at East Runton in their deck chairs, watching over a thousand children playing on the beach. God brought to the minds of both of them, independently but instantaneously, the same words of Christ: "Other sheep I have which are not of this fold, them also I must bring." They got up from their chairs immediately, and went up into the village to look for the largest house in it. Having found it, they wrote a letter to its owner, whose name they did not know, and delivered it by hand.

It transpired that the owner of the house was a judge. His reply was further proof of the authenticity of the call they had been given a few days before on the beach. "Yes," he replied, "you may use the house for a CSSM party"—and added that it brought memories of his childhood days when he joined in a CSSM beach mission and responded to the message.

The call of God is not, of course, exclusively to any one race or group. Increasingly in recent years He has been calling men and women in the so-called non-Christian lands to serve Him there—and in other places. The story of one young Ceylonese shows how profound an impression such a call can make.

This young man came to faith in Christ at the age of fifteen, while a pupil at the "Harrow of Ceylon", as a result of a private conversation with a Scripture Union staff worker. The boy's mother was a doctor and a Buddhist; his father was a very nominal Christian. The boy, however, entered into a real assurance of Christ, and became a dynamic influence on his fellows.

He came to Britain to study, first at Cambridge and then at London University, and qualified as a doctor. During his time at London he was elected President of the London Inter-faculty Christian Union and served on the student executive committee of the Inter-Varsity Fellowship. His influence on many other students, of all races, was profound.

He has now returned to Ceylon where, as a young doctor, he is trying to get together university students to meet for Christian study and fellowship. The call of God, through the Scriptures or through human agencies, is no static force.

Constantly He speaks to Christians whose ears are open to hear, to point them to new tasks, new openings and new opportunities. It is this call—this true vocation—which turns employees into partners, and toil into joyful service.

CHAPTER 6

For All the People

The Central Hall, Westminster was packed to the rafters, and downstairs an overflow meeting was itself overflowing. Hundreds of young people had been turned away and hundreds more had not bothered coming when they had heard that all the reserved tickets were gone. In the main hall 2,700 young people, mostly teenagers, had their eyes riveted on the floodlit platform, where a beat group was pouring out electronic sound by the millions of decibels.

A casual observer might have been forgiven some scepticism if he had been told that this was a religious meeting; but it was. The huge crowds of teenagers had not come to hear a pop idol but to consider a Christian viewpoint on personal relationships, under the intriguing title "Hitting it off". An imaginative soundstrip, a panel, a roving mike to discover the audience's views, on the spot interviews and a short closing talk made up the evening—plus, of course, the music of "The Joystrings", the Salvation Army's own beat group. The theme of the evening was this: that one cannot rightly relate to other people (individually, or as a group, or as nations) until one is rightly related to God. The audience (one could not possibly describe it as a "congregation") went away more thoughtfully than they came.

That is an example of the way in which the Scripture Union has adapted its approach to meet the needs of today. More than any other religious organisation that one can name it has been brave enough to tackle the 1960's on their own ground and on their own terms. For a movement with so venerable and honourable a history, this has required courage and vision.

Of course, the Bible reading system is still the heart of of the SU's ministry, as it must be. But even that has been widened in its appeal, as we have seen. The other aspects of the movement's work, and especially those parts relating to children and young people, have been positively transformed since the Second World War.

In Croydon, for instance, there now stands a fine modern Christian bookshop run by the Scripture Union. It represents the fifth stage of growth from a humble effort at distributing Christian literature over fifty years ago—from a stall in the market—on a site only a few hundred yards from the present bookshop. The Scripture Union did not enter the scene in any official capacity until 1964, but now a shop which bears comparison for design and efficiency with any in this flourishing shopping centre is meeting a growing demand in the area.

This is the newest of the SU bookshops. The oldest, and largest, is in Wigmore Street, in London's West End, and must be one of the finest evangelical bookshops in Europe. Operating on three floors, and with departments covering current books, paperbacks, secondhand books, records and music, filmstrips and tape recordings, projectors and portable organs and children's books and Sunday school supplies, it is a Christian ministry on its own. There are also SU bookshops in Manchester and Glasgow.

From the offices in Marylebone Lane—just a couple of blocks away from the London SU bookshop—the work of the SU is directed. Here the notes and Scripture passages are planned and edited, the various periodicals and magazines are produced, and the publishing of the range of books and booklets under the Scripture Union imprint is carried on. A staff of over a hundred, led by an executive team under a General Secretary, cope with all this work.

A glance through the literature emanating from SU headquarters would be sufficient to verify that here is a movement genuinely concerned to be up-to-date and relevant, while keeping faithful to the biblical Gospel. This is true, for instance, of the "Wake up to the Bible" drive launched in November 1965, and intended as the first shot in a campaign to enlist half a million new Bible readers. The slogan was superb, with just the right double-meaning, and easily memorised. The posters and leaflets were eye-catching and simple. The special booklet *To Get You Started* was an admirable example of how to package a first class product.

We have already mentioned the Sunday school department. Anyone who bases his ideas of a modern Sunday school on recollections of his own childhood more than ten years ago is sadly mistaken. Things have changed.

By well-produced literature, teachers' notes, take-home leaflets and other practical aids, and through teachers' training week-ends and training soundstrips the SU Sunday school experts have dedicated themselves to transforming the Church's work among children. It is a slow transformation, but they are winning.

The days when Sunday school consisted of a few Victorian hymns, half a dozen choruses, the "collection" and then a twenty minute talk by the teacher are, if not entirely gone, certainly numbered. Visual aids, activity sessions and projects have made the teaching child-centred rather than teacher-centred, and changed drudgery into pleasure.

One little known department at SU headquarters is the "Modern Communications Unit". The pioneer of this work is now a producer with the BBC, and his successor came to Scripture Union from an Independent Television Company. That will indicate something of the standards the unit has come to set itself. This unit produces the SU's range of filmstrips and soundstrips (filmstrips with tape-recorded commentaries) and other visual aids.

The ministry of the Scripture Union is now, as several stories in this book have demonstrated, genuinely world-wide. It publishes Bible reading aids in 148 languages and has full-time staff representatives in 34 countries. One incident a year or so ago illustrates just how far the Scripture Union Bible reading scheme has penetrated. A supply plane was making a parachute drop of goods and presents for Christmas to a remote Eskimo settlement within the Arctic circle. It made several trial runs, and then dropped nine large parcels . . . which floated slowly earthwards and finally disappeared with a splash down a water-hole. There were miles of unbroken ice around, but with uncanny accuracy the parcels managed to land in the one and only patch of unfrozen water. Only one parcel was retrieved, and that contained 400 Scripture Union reading cards for the local people.

However, the story is not quite as impressive as it sounds, as the cards were unreadable and had to be reprinted!

It must be stressed that all this activity is intended to serve one simple aim: to make the Bible and its message clear and plain to the men and women of Britain (and the world) in the mid-twentieth century. The idea is not to build an SU empire, or create a mammoth business venture, but to tell modern man that the word of God has something to say to him that he ignores at his infinite loss, and to help him to get to grips with it.

That it is succeeding to a large extent is demonstrated by the comments of a young man, and a young woman, both very much products of their age.

The young man, a science student whose faith has only come alive in the last year or so, writes: "I started to read the Bible regularly. I chose a New Testament letter and started reading a few verses each day. After about a week I found that I was getting bogged down and not making much progress at all. For me, as an inexperienced Christian, it was not easy just to open the Bible and immediately find something relevant to me.

"Some time afterwards I was given a set of Scripture Union *Daily Bread* notes and I started using them. I found they made all the difference to my Bible reading and it really did begin to mean something to me.

"This, I think, was for three reasons.

"Firstly, because I was encouraged and guided to *pray*—that God would speak to me through the passages I read, and that he would show me how the principles I learned should be made effective in my life.

"Secondly, because the written commentary helped me

to sort out the important, basic lessons from what I was reading.

"Thirdly, the passages are chosen in such a way that they follow through a complete story or letter and hence there is a continuity between one day's reading and the next."

The young woman tells a very similar story.

"Although I was a Christian, and brought up in a Christian home, I regarded Bible reading as a very irksome task, often not understanding what I was reading and getting nothing from it. However, for some years now I have been taking the Scripture Union notes and it is now a real pleasure to read the Bible . . . The notes do shed light on difficult passages and many times I have been greatly blessed and encouraged through systematic daily reading of the Scriptures . . ."

It is worth noting what these two people say of their own unaided attempts at Bible reading: "I was getting bogged down . . . it was not easy to find something relevant . . . very irksome . . . not understanding and getting nothing from it." Modern man, like his less well educated forebears, needs help in reading the Bible, even when he uses a modern translation (a practice strongly commended by the Scripture Union for some years now). It is not enough to give him a Bible and expect him to have an immediate breakthrough to full understanding of it. He needs help, and it is precisely this help, at many different levels, that the Scripture Union sets out to give. Its million and a half members world-wide obviously find it just what they need.

CHAPTER 7

Epilogue: For You?

Dennis came with a crowd of fellows on a week's cruise up the Thames organised by a Scripture Union worker. He was conspicuous by his energy and zest during the daytime activities and by his absence when the time came for evening prayers. When this had happened for four consecutive evenings, the leader decided to take steps to see that, like it or not, Dennis would be at prayers the following night.

So it came about that Dennis, a rowdy seventeen-year-old, became an unwilling hearer of the Word. One assumes he reckoned it a small price to pay for what was proving a terrific holiday, and, to give him credit, he caused no trouble during the short Bible reading and prayers each night for the rest of the week.

When Saturday came the party broke up, and the leader never expected to hear of Reluctant Dennis again.

However, some seven years later he was invited to take the Sunday services at a little church away in the country. He was welcomed at the door by a church officer who conducted him to the vestry. "I expect you are wondering how we came to invite you here to preach?"

The worker nodded.

"It was our secretary's suggestion. He has often told us

about you and your work. He speaks very highly of you and of the way you introduced him to God."

A moment later the church secretary entered the room. It was Dennis. Apparently on that Thames cruise seven years before he had been listening rather more closely than most people imagined. An interest in the Bible and a longing for God were born in that reluctant hearer, which later bore fruit in a life given to God and His service.

This is typical of the way the Bible "gets under our skins". It is an incredibly hard book to ignore once one has made its acquaintance in a real and vivid way. From the workman in Spurgeon's Tabernacle a hundred years ago who was converted through hearing the great preacher declaim the words "Behold the lamb of God which taketh away the sin of the world" to test the acoustics; to the famous pop-singer who told the author how the Bible gripped him as he read and re-read the New Testament in the New English Bible, and how this was the beginning of true faith in Christ for Him: the Bible has a tremendously penetrative message.

We have seen this in so many of the accounts in this book of journeys into faith. It has not been any famous preacher or brilliant eloquence that has persuaded them but, most frequently, the irresistible authority and magnetism of Jesus Christ as He is seen in the New Testament. This is His work in men's lives, and the Bible's role in it is to reveal Him in an authoritative and trustworthy way, in the context of God's dealings with man and man's need for redemption.

A survey quoted by Scripture Union last year revealed that only two in every five of *regular churchgoers* read the

Bible themselves. They hear it read in church, they may even believe in its importance and value; but they do not actually read it. If this is true (and there is no evidence to cast doubt on it) then probably many of those who are reading this book never, or hardly ever, read the Bible themselves. Like the young man and woman quoted in the last chapter, they may well have made a half-hearted try, but found it "heavy going", "very irksome", not easily understood.

One hopes that, if nothing else, this little book will have demonstrated the power of the Bible to penetrate to the heart of the matter and bring life, comfort, guidance, strength or correction where they are needed. One hopes that it will have caused some to ask whether they are missing something good and worthwhile by leaving their Bibles unread. One even hopes that some may be stimulated to give regular Bible reading—the Scripture Union way!—a really serious try. If so, it is probably worth pointing out that the introductory readings *Invitation to Live* are designed to get new readers started, and can be strongly recommended. So can a good, legible Bible, preferably in an intelligible modern translation such as the Revised Standard Version.

But the really important advice for the would-be Bible reader is that he should read "regularly, believingly and expectantly". We saw how these qualities characterised the readers whom God most clearly helped and guided through their daily readings.

"Regularly" means just what it says, but preferably daily. The Bereans were commended by Paul because they "searched the Scriptures daily", to check on the accuracy of his preaching. There is a discipline here, especially in these frantic days; but it is a positive and rewarding one.

"Believingly" means that we read with faith—in God, in His Word, and in His faithfulness. We put our trust in Him; we believe that what He has inspired and preserved is true and trustworthy; and we rely on Him to mean what He says and do what He promises.

"Expectantly" simply means that we come eagerly to the Bible, expecting to hear God's voice, looking for His Word to us in this or that situation, taking time to dig into the Scriptures for the pure gold that we know is there for those who sincerely seek it.

Regularly, believingly, expectantly: that is how the people whose stories are told in this book came to the Bible. But the message of this remarkable revelation of God is not just for them, nor any other restricted group: not just for the pious, or the religious, or the intelligent, or the gullible. God loved the *world*, and gave His Son for it. His book, too, is for all the people.